About the Author

Elinor Peace Bailey was born in the midwest and grew up in Scarsdale, New York. She attended the Tyler School of Fine Arts at Temple University and after joining the Mormon Church continued her art education at the Brigham Young University where she received her B.S. degree in art education. In addition, she has studied at Parson's School of Design, the Art Student's League and San Jose State.

She has created several doll patterns, including her popular Victorian Doll, plus a book of poetry and drawings, and three books with Virginia Robertson of the Osage County Quilt Factory.

Elinor lives in the San Francisco Bay area and teaches dollmaking near her home and throughout the United States and Canada. In addition to being an exciting teacher, often credited with offering new dimensions to women's lives, she is a wife and mother of a large family, nine in all.

Her daughter Laura at the age of 13 wrote that her mother's "main theme is to help women recognize their own worth ... My mother has always encouraged me to love myself and to be who I want to be ... When I grow up I plan to be an artist ... I know I will be a strong woman; my mother has taught me how."

Dedication

*It goes without saying that no book could be without
the help of an excellent editor. This I have had in Evelyn Metzger.
Thanks to her I can dedicate this book to the people
who have known me best. My parents who nurtured my art even
when it was inconvenient. My husband who encouraged
me to be myself and my children who have been both
a delight and a trial. There are many others who have nourished
what was in me, and to all of them I give my thanks.*

Acknowledgments

*I wish to acknowledge the following people
for their kind assistance in writing this book:*
David Berg *of Sacramento California
for his beautiful black and white photographs of my studio.
The doll artists and students who shared
their imaginative renditions of the modular doll with me.
My son* **Isaac** *who printed the photographs
taken in Kalispel, Montana, of the doll class
by Joan Hodgeboom, the owner of the Quilt Gallery.
My father,* **Robert McDonald,** *for his listening ear
and discerning mind. He was a consultant on the book also.
Thanks to all of the listening ears and willing hands.*

Elinor Peace Bailey

Mother Plays With Dolls

...and finds an important key
to unlocking creativity

EPM Publications, Inc.
McLean, Virginia

Library of Congress Cataloging-in-Publication Data

Bailey, Elinor Peace.
    Mother plays with dolls . . . and finds an important key to
unlocking creativity / Elinor Peace Bailey.
      p. cm.
    ISBN 0-939009-39-0
    1. Bailey, Elinor Peace—Themes, motives, 2. Dollmaking.
I. Title.
NK4894.2.B35A4   1990
745.592'21—dc20   90-3210
                                            CIP

EPM Publications, Inc., 1003 Turkey Run Road
  McLean, VA 22101

Printed in U.S.A. by Progress Printing

Illustrations by Elinor Peace Bailey
Cover and book design by Tom Huestis
Color photography by Lise Metzger
Black/white photography by David Berg and Isaac Bailey

Contents

The
Magic of the Doll:
An
Introductory Note

All over the world people are collecting dolls—antique bisques, limited edition porcelains; decorative cloth dolls; paper, plastic and composition dolls that remind them pleasantly of their youths; foreign dolls, even fetish dolls. Many of today's artists who make only one-of-a-kind dolls cannot make enough of them to satisfy their markets.

In our country doll collecting has become the leading hobby surpassing even stamp collecting. What is there about the representation of a human form, however whimsical, that makes people want to possess it? What magic is transferred into that form that has given it power over so many?

The question is not easily answered. Many doll collectors seem to find in them a genteel reminder of their child-hoods. All kinds of fantasies can be aroused by dolls. Some-times divine powers can be invoked through a doll, and it can be seen as a benediction on the households of those who have the faith to receive it. Since his earliest history man has changed the abstract into simple forms and given them the power to heal and enlighten.

All this and more lend magic to dolls. I have written this book to help others explore this healing, nurturing resource and to encourage them in the making of their own magic.

1.
Why This Mother Plays With Dolls

Language, an indispensable element of any person's self-expression, can take many forms: music, dance, painting, sculpture, writing, speaking, a mere body stance, or an angry face. How ever it is proffered, over a microphone or through "a still small voice," it is essential. Each of us must find his own language and leave his mark on whatever environment he finds himself in. As for me, I found my language in dolls.

As a child I said enough, a great deal I am told. But as an adolescent, I appeared to be unable to reach other people with my words. Frustrated and lonely, unable to get what I needed, my language communicated more and more hostility, and people withdrew from me in order not to be overwhelmed by my need for love and my awkward and overbearing attempts to get it.

In that state, I married a man, Gary, who could see through the protective melodrama and accept me as I was. In no time, two step-children and one kid who adopted our family plus six children of our own had me buried in nine other egos from my own.

The children came innocently leaving their messages at my feet. First Greg, eight, and Cindy, five, Gary's children.

At twenty-three, I was far less prepared for mothering than they were for being children. I look back and marvel now that we became friends. Greg and I have a mutual respect and Cindy is indeed my daughter.

Evalyn was the first born to me. She was and remains the family princess. It is impossible not to love Evalyn. Then came Ross, my perfect son, brilliant and self directed—a star out of my orbit. We are sometimes strange to one another. These first two of my own were easy enough, but then came Isaac, an upside-down explosion. Charming, hanging by one leg. He plucks a rose to study it by himself and understands the whole world, but he will not do his math.

Maureen has always seemed to pull to herself every needed thing. As she felt a need, she filled it. She is a bit of a dictator now, but I predict she will manage us all with a fine-honed skill when she is a bit wiser.

Laura and I love the same things. There was bound to be one among so many who would follow in my steps. When she was ten there was a poem. When she was eleven she dressed like me for Halloween. My studio was never safe from her projects and messes. Any irritation that might arise was dispersed when I was brought to marvel at what she had made. She will do glorious things when she gains full control of her skills.

Alberto, the kid who adopted our family, delivered himself to us when he was nearly grown, at about the same time that George was born. Alberto came needing a place to rest and re-group. Because he needed, we loved; and for this we have been amply repaid. Perhaps we have taught Alberto a bit about how to love and how not to be afraid of losing love.

From the time George was old enough to hold more than one thing in his grasp he has collected things in series. The trucks and the cars stretched in a line from one end of the house to the other, then came the Garbage Pail Kids and baseball cards and a seemingly endless stream of little plastic figures. A bony yet cuddly kid, last to arrive.

I count them nine in all and each has expanded my understanding. In addition there are also seven grandchildren. The expansion continues.

Despite the demands of motherhood and even though I had gained more patience, I found myself stubbornly unable to give up my painting. No one asked me to, of course;

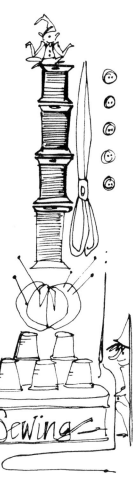

Sewing

but so many other young mothers whom I met seemed to be willing to postpone their own lives to rear their children. I could not.

I discovered fabric one year while substitute-teaching at the Alameda County Juvenile Hall. A friend of mine was the home economics teacher there. Over the years she had received numerous donations of old fabric scraps which she shared with me. As I pawed through them, the patterns and textures reached out to me like welcoming hands and pulled me into their depths. One piece in juxtaposition to another. Here was instant excitement. I began to put them together in fiber paintings.

The process of combining fabrics was spontaneous. I could stitch while riding in a car, or sitting through elementary school concerts. I actually looked forward to long, drawn-out meetings. My artistic voice, which had been confined to what I could squeeze into my time at home, began stepping out. I began feeding what appeared to be an insatiable hunger. Still as much as my fiber work filled my head and my walls with language, there were few who were listening. Most of my friends did not understand, and the kind of unconditional acceptance that I apparently needed only increased. Finally, Mary Beth Cragun, a friend and a member of my church, said five of the most important words ever spoken to me—"I want to commission you"—and my world changed.

TO ONE WHO HAS SEEN AND UNDERSTOOD

Tread gently when you walk into my life
For around the body of my soul I have gathered
Fragile gossamer, to the floor, of little lies—
Not to deceive you—but to protect me.

Do not pull at them to render my soul naked
For they hide truths I have not yet the strength to face.
And when they are gone I may perish.
In the cold realities of your judgment I may die.

But let me stand protected yet awhile.
Talk to me in love, and when I am secure in that
Those lies will fall away as un-needed peel
Revealing the fruit, the feast.

I made a hanging for her, adapted from a pattern in a *Vogue* catalogue. I included a family portrait in applique which led to another commission for a friend of hers, a bride and groom pillow, and five full-size family album quilts. I was on my way.

It wasn't long before I got involved with a once-a-year boutique group. It was scheduled for the Christmas season, and I spent the entire summer dreaming up new ideas. I used to play a game with myself called "How can I make this thing out of cloth?" I scoured small shops for good ideas done badly which were my all-time favorite kinds of ideas. I stacked up piles of holiday magazines for inspiration. As ideas flooded in, October approached. Increasingly I found that the dolls I made sold in a flash, and I even had a collector or two who stood at the door to be first in line to buy. Soon I was receiving commissions throughout the year.

Finally I had found my language. The dolls brought me the love that I hungered for. The audience I began to acquire through them permitted me to be myself. The dolls,

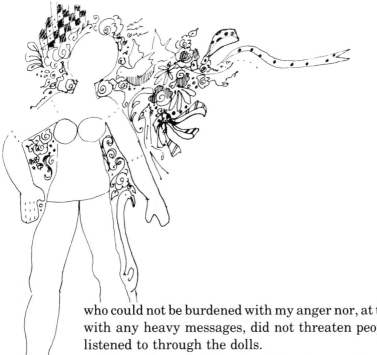

who could not be burdened with my anger nor, at this point, with any heavy messages, did not threaten people. I was listened to through the dolls.

What a time of celebration it is when you finally find a way to reach out to another person, even to dolls, the objects of your creation. One of the decided advantages in becoming a dollmaker is that all that talking to yourself you once did can be directed instead to your dolls.

"You know," I said to Hattie, when I was sewing her, "You know, when I was in college I planned to be a great artist, like Matisse or Picasso or Rembrandt. I thought that would justify everything—my passion for color, pattern and the human image. If I were a great artist, I could do art all the time; who would dare question?"

Hattie listened as she had been made to do. "But then," I said, "I saw the truth. My work was never going to deal with the monumental." She smiled, or so I thought. "So I just made live babies and tried to be content in domesticity. But sometimes, even artists who deal with little things have a passion, and even a small gift may prove uncontainable." Hattie sighed. Had she been able, she would have asked how an artistic expression, even a small one, gets out. That's when this poem sprang forth—a kind of Greek apology to explain why mother plays with dolls.

THE DOLL

I plucked her out of the air
And there she was, wonderful
And she had her own presence
And she spoke to me
And we were one, the doll and I.

"Absurd," said they,
"A doll?"
"People over ten don't play with dolls."
But I could only see my pleasure in her
And decided, after all these years of listening to
*   other voices, not to hear.*

Now some, more profound than I,
Have drawn from within themselves far greater
*   pleasures than stuffed fantasies.*
I know that.
But within me there was this doll
And she would out.

Now perhaps in my own beginning, somewhere behind a
*   star,*
He thought my self and brought me forth
Not from nothingness, my essence ever having existed,
But ordered me born again.
Was He as proud and pleased, knowing He had others made
*   more impressive? Perhaps.*

Now He and I have done another thing together,
And If I, then others, have gathered from creations
loveliness—things not grand but small—
Shall I, knowing your capacity, reach out to you?
When within you lies a garden
Needing only to be tended.

2.
A Way to See Who You Are

Once in a flight of fancy I saw myself as having a quantity of rooms within me, very much like an old Victorian house. As I wandered through the house I found that I had access to only some of the rooms. Some of the doors to the rooms were locked against my entry, as if they held memories that I could not face, or secrets that I was not prepared to know. I realized that in order for me to free myself of the fear that I felt when I thought of entering those rooms I must embrace and acknowledge all that I was and use my inner diversity and the richness of my life experience and, yes, even its pain. I knew that if I were to be of use to myself and others, every room in that house must be known.

THE HOUSE

I enter in within the wall.
The rooms each welcome or repel.
I close the doors. I lock the cupboard.
Part of the house I never enter.
It is black there, and full of unspoken fears.

My nursery, where I draw and color and dream,
I am too often called away from.
I must justify every moment you know.
Even in bed I am only partly satisfied.
Part of me cannot look and know that I have sex.

elinor peace bailey

I am necessarily drawn to the toilet.
For I am human and my body is what it is and
*   must relieve itself.*
What I see of me is not always lovely—tee-dum
What I see of me is not always what is.

Anyone can go into the parlor.
Anyone can speak there, but not necessarily her
*   thoughts.*
I think I like the kitchen well enough;
From this place I gather and nourish.
So good am I in this room, that some do not wish me
*   to leave.*

In the attic there is the rich collective—the
*   history, the past.*
I open and look, from here I have direction,
*   perspective and laughter.*
It is spring, my dear;
Open to me every cupboard, every hidden door.
Free me to walk through all of the house.
Give me access to all of my sweet self.

When you are a little crazy it's helpful to find a way of explaining you to you. I have always felt safer and more complete when I could crawl into a package of words. It is as if they held me together and defined my limits. So when I discovered transactional analysis I got all excited. First of all, the word transactional contains the word transaction and that implies making deals and, second, I loved the idea that I contained more than one person within me. That made me a crowd and talking to myself became a great deal more like talking to an audience, and there is nothing I like better than talking to an audience.

So, in order for this book to be of use to those of you who read it, let's talk a bit about the crowd within you. It is my understanding that transactional theorists divide each of us into six distinct individuals. The interaction among all these characters can be referred to as transactions. "Such a deal I'll make for you" or "Who's in charge here?"

I think of these individuals as existing in layers. The first layer is the child, which is itself divided into "the natural child," "the adjusted child," and "the little professor." Within the "natural child" is found the primal emo-

15

tions and urges such as sensuality, spontaneity, creativity, anger and fear. The "adjusted child" is the sum of her reactions to her life's experience. This area holds all the survival techniques that it has been necessary to acquire. The "adjusted child" can be negatively patterned and can be a source of psychological illness if survival has meant acquiring self-destructive adjustments.

"The little professor" is the seat of intuition and knowing. To some this part is connected to what Carl Gustav Jung referred to as the "collective unconscious," [all human knowing both past and present]. This area of the inner child is an extremely valuable resource.

The second layer is "the parent." "The parent" consists of two parts: "the nurturing parent" who cares for and encourages the child and "the critical parent" who limits and warns the child, sometimes for good and sometimes not. This layer represents the relationships established between the child and the primary adult caretaker. The interactions of childhood are taped and played over and over again even when the adults in question and the child have been separated for a very long time. So if your parents were your very best cheerleaders and now they are gone, the happy voices of their approval are still there in your head. Unfortunately, however, if they were your worst critics that tape remains as well. Most of us do not monitor our behaviors and simply accept these interactions, or more properly these transactions, without question, which often means that we go through life on a predetermined path, allowing little growth or maturation to occur.

The remaining layer of the personality is "the adult," who, in the mature individual, mediates transactions between the parent and the child, keeping one layer from dominating or tyrannizing the other. "The adult" determines what is real, calming fears and modifying behaviors, and ideally is reality-based. One hopes that every part of us will work toward helping us realize our full potential and make a maximum contribution to the universe.

I have used the doll as a tool to free my personality. Because dolls are so wonderfully without consequence, they have enormous potential for amusing their makers and, in the process, for offering insight. Something so benign can take the danger out of imagining. Playing with dolls is a safe way to explore change and make discoveries; and play, after all, is the very center of the creative act.

16

3.
Playing With a Group

I travel a great deal, back and forth across the country, wearing the clothes of my trade. Since there are very few cloth dollmakers who travel on planes to teach other cloth dollmakers how to make dolls, I have had to invent the clothes of my trade and left to my own devices I have not made them of blue serge.

People sometimes comment on my clothes rather apologetically. They say things like, "I hope you don't mind my staring." Or they whisper to one another as if I didn't know that my appearance was exotic. I just smile and tell them that I don't dress the way I do to be ignored. I do get a few laughs on planes and in the streets. I have friends who like to walk behind me and watch the reactions of people as I pass, and, as I often tell, my kids dress up like me for Halloween. Now, this indicates that for me play remains an important commitment in life.

Some people believe that play is the business of childhood and should be left as a pleasant memory, but I believe that play, a seemingly purposeless act done without fear of judgment, is the thinking generated by the inner child. I do not believe that the creative act can be approached without unfettered play, like building sandcastles without worrying about their being washed away.

But time and life separate us from our childhood and the dilemma that the adult faces is how to maintain the spirit of the child along with adult judgment, facility and images. How can we justify time spent in play as adults? Where do we get permission?

Over the centuries women have put aside their own childhoods and taken on children. If they played at all they centered their play on their children. When the children left there were the grandchildren to care for or simply empty nests to mourn. Was it only the passing of their children into adulthood or were they suffering an even greater loss, the passing of their own inner childhoods?

Women have always facilitated male childhood, taking care of male needs, mothering and even referring to men as "little boys." Football games on TV, boats, RVs and fishing poles are "Daddy's toys." Where, pray tell, are Mommy's?

Now, there are plenty of problems in today's world waiting for creative solutions. Plenty of need for both playful women and playful men to put down the burden of too much structure and to think beyond the traditional. So why does a woman's job description still allow childhood only in others? Why must her actions be centered in practicality in order to be justified? Without play for the sake of play there can be little daring, little change or fresh vision. "And a little child shall lead them," may well refer to our own inner child. For the child within believes, follows whims, and sees few impediments or barriers. This is the child to whom we must all turn if the world is to be made new.

As adults we call every new thought into question, holding each idea to the light of day. Frequently in our transactional sandwich the only part of us justified in the world is the inner parent who continually nags, "What is it for? Does it fit? What shall I do with it? Or will it be approved of?" Thus we constrict the child within and question her ideas and creations to death. With all these tapes playing over and over, how can we see things anew or create a new order?

And yet the problems of our world demand the fresh vision and new insights inspired by play. That aimless messing with stuff and ideas is at the very center of creativity, and dolls and dollmaking can be a delightful key to it all. What simpler symbol of the inner child? Defined simply as the personification of material, the doll can be the ultimate sandbox where one can do as she pleases. Who could care? People, endless streams of people, dancing in your head, can do as they like, look as you wish them to look and articulate your dreams. Surely a doll, who pretends to no importance, can be as we please her to be.

You may have noticed that most commercial doll patterns are neither surprising nor unpredictable. They are sweet and we love them, but there are few jaw droppers among them. I believe that this conformity has much to do with the inability of many dollmakers to find the time to do a doll for no reason at all. But if every idea has to be marketable, then we may miss the bits of craziness, or flights of fancy that might make a difference. In order to conjure up a new image the kid inside has to be invited out to play. This requires sacrificing one of our greatest fears: the fear of being wrong.

THE WINDOW

Barrier, sometimes undeclared,
There it is, keeping me in or out.
Keeping the rain from my face
And the cold—But alas, isolating me too,
        from the spring breeze
And baking me with the summer heat.

So fling it wide from time to time.
Let me risk the cold and rain
So that I am not robbed
Of the gentle welcome spring.

Now, if our inner child, that reservoir of spontaneity who sees the world anew, is cut off, who brings the fairy dust to our work? Could it be a critical parent tape full of little fears that puts us all in boxes and keeps us from risking? Considering the scheme of things—power politics, world hunger, personal violence, and eternal philosophical matters—the doll is nothing. A dollmaker ought to be left to play out this absurdity, and even to treasure the results. But the commercial dollmaker has to lay her money down, money being society's measure of importance, and thus she pays an even higher price in loss of imagination. Will it sell? Oh my dear, what a heavy chain.

PLAY

I took the fabric out to play today,
And sitting there among the scraps, I had a thought.
But put it safely from me.
When the inner critic, with an outraged expression
Showed me how simply absurd it was to think that
such a little mind as mine could be capable
of seeing what had not yet been seen,
I, wishing to be safe from judgment,
And seeing the danger of that original planted in
my path,
Took up the scraps and put them neatly by in eye-
pleasing stacks
For another, more gifted than myself, to make a
masterpiece.
As for me, I would take the children for a walk
and then make dinner.

So the doll, that errant bit of childhood whimsey, the ultimate sandbox, can be the symbol, the place to return to. Gathered in her little-girl dreams a woman can find the strength to imagine. I am constantly on the lookout for a group of players. Bunches of people who will play have a kind of built-in permission that is catching, and people with similar interests are bound to come in flocks. In the case of 20 or so ladies from the Hayward, California area this flock has taken on the name of the "Flying

Phoebes." They are named after one of my dolls. The doll was inspired by a paper airplane my son Isaac threatened to throw at the Bishop one Sunday morning.

The Flying Phoebes meet once a month to learn more about cloth dollmaking and because I am a contributing member we sometimes take on odd assignments, such as Friendship Dolls. They were conceived as an exercise in relinquishing control of a creation to someone else and working with a given, over which you have no control. Something like the paper folding game we used to play as children. Remember the accordion-pleated paper strip on which you drew a head and passed it along to the next person who drew a neck? The next person drew the next part and so on until the whole figure was completed. Finally it was unfolded to reveal the surprise monster.

To begin a Friendship Doll each of us made a body, either from our own design or from a pattern. Each doll was brought to the January meeting in a paper bag. We drew numbers to establish to whom we would pass our doll. That person was to do the face, the next person, the hair. After that came underwear, clothing, accessories and finally the environment. The results were amazing and outrageous. We had sent our pieces out into the world to receive the world's imprint and they came back to us as total surprises. Every step left fewer and fewer choices because once the face was applied and the wigging done, the personality of the doll had emerged pretty decisively.

When I first considered what doll body I would take to the meeting, I knew it would be original. I was shopping in one of my favorite haunts in Castro Valley called Bolt's

End when I came across an apple green stripe, as unlikely a fabric for a being as I could imagine. I brought it home to think about it. I loved it. Finally, with the deadline approaching, I re-produced the picture in my head on paper, and then on cloth. She was delicate and nymphlike. I could not imagine what would be done with her at the next stage. But I did know that whoever took her home was going to have a challenge in creating the face. And the hair? From the moment she went into the hands of her face mother I did not see her again until the meeting in June when she arrived with her staring appliqued eyes, dark pursed lips, blooming rose-colored ribbon yarn hair, black lace G-string and camisole, a fuchsia nylon robe, black feather scuffs and a black feather boa. She was marvelous! I gave her an environment of lamé pillows. She would recline with her volume of Proust somewhere in Paris where she no doubt has a salon. Artists gather there and call her only "Henriette." She is an artist's model and an intellectual, much loved and admired.

All the dolls had their stories, their struggles and their characters, developed as they passed from hand to hand. Finally they come to rest with their first makers who had created their bodies. From these original makers they received their final definitions.

The value of such an exercise is that it stretches us. There is group support for the play and success is having a good time, a good laugh. To operate as a creative individual in a cooperative setting can be a spiritual experience, for blending what we are with others is finding a new kind of belonging. Such blending requires a sense of humor because humor gives us perspective. It has long been a tool of survival for the human race. Humor aids confrontation with reality and the absurdity of our time-centered lives. With humor we can honestly face our helplessness in this universe. Best to laugh, best to cooperate with one another and to make a choir of our little voices. Best to see our flaws and fears as common to all.

Other kinds of group play can produce wonderful things too. For several years I have included a Fabric Improvisation class as part of my classroom offerings. The students bring their talents and gifts to class, such as the ability to piece, or collect, or do fine needlework, plus their old buttons, stacks of fabrics and kitsch. I bring my gifts: my ability to draw, my intuition, my love of color, and my understanding of machine applique. We take all that has been gathered at this chance meeting and make something together. When it works, this is what is known as a synergetic experience, one in which we can do more in combination than what we could do separately. Wonderful things have come out of this class, and to the degree that I can be guided intuitively to match the expectations of the people I work with each piece is markedly different and often far beyond my personal ability to produce. I have used this same approach in a "Design Your Own Doll" class with equally wonderful results.

It is obvious that when the ego barriers come tumbling down in such classes more is shared than just a creative experience. Long-held secrets come tumbling out and life struggles are discussed. The dolls and the use of intuition make this kind of contact possible. One woman played out her anger at her mother. She announced that she was going to give her the doll she was making, and then when she saw that it was going to be a lovely piece she withdrew the gift noting her mother's lack of appreciation of something really nice. Another brought her mother with her. Understanding flowed between them. The love of the mother was reflected in the daughter. I was able to remark upon that.

While teaching in the east, I met a woman of about 35 who was taking a class. She was smartly dressed and very attractive. Bouncy as a little girl, her conversation indicated that she was bright and had a multitude of interests. I always ask my students about themselves. This young woman had no family of her own and was living with her mother. She had never married. I made a joke about her being picky and she laughed. I asked her what she did for a living, expecting her to tell me that she did something extremely demanding and exciting that would explain her lack of interest in having a family of her own. She told me that she was a teacher's aide for kids with educational handicaps. I asked her about her education and learned that she had never finished college. Throughout this interview we were making dolls and I was moving about the classroom trouble shooting and giving tips on construction. But I was curious. This woman was not consistent. What I felt about her did not fit with the biographical stuff she was sharing. She told me that she had worked in New York City. She had had a good job there and an exciting life but had quit and come home because she felt inadequate in the position though her boss thought she was quite adequate. Then the story unfolded. Her father, now deceased, had been an abusive parent. He had heeped psychological abuse on all three of his daughters. The other two had distanced themselves from that environment, but this girl had headed home to live with a passive mother who had never defended her as a child and for whom she had a great deal of anger. Their house was the scene of the abuse. She had come back to it to hide, angry and hurt. Tears welled up in her eyes as the questions unveiled the realities.

I held her and then suggested it was time for some help. I advised her to find a female therapist whom she could trust and who could help her deal with her anger and to get on with her life. Her "adjusted child" was so badly beaten up, and her "parent tape" so abusive that she would have a great deal of rebuilding to do. It was best to start now.

This kind of play therapy happens all the time in my classroom, and from what I have gathered from other recreational sewing teachers it happens in theirs too. An atmosphere of total freedom becomes real here. Women who are unable to allow their minds to frolic in any other setting find themselves permitted and encouraged to return to the playing mode. The dolls that they dream up are three dimensional and real and true reflections of themselves.

Well! Will you look at that!

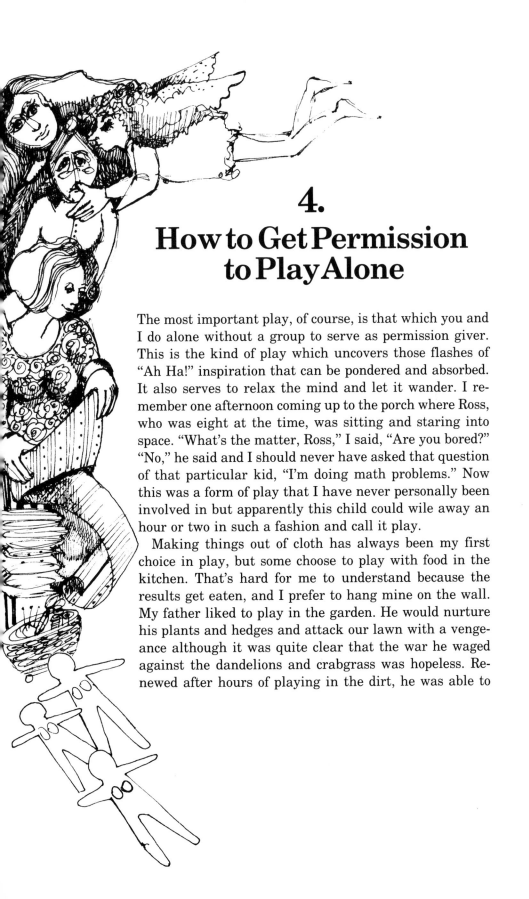

4.
How to Get Permission to Play Alone

The most important play, of course, is that which you and I do alone without a group to serve as permission giver. This is the kind of play which uncovers those flashes of "Ah Ha!" inspiration that can be pondered and absorbed. It also serves to relax the mind and let it wander. I remember one afternoon coming up to the porch where Ross, who was eight at the time, was sitting and staring into space. "What's the matter, Ross," I said, "Are you bored?" "No," he said and I should never have asked that question of that particular kid, "I'm doing math problems." Now this was a form of play that I have never personally been involved in but apparently this child could wile away an hour or two in such a fashion and call it play.

Making things out of cloth has always been my first choice in play, but some choose to play with food in the kitchen. That's hard for me to understand because the results get eaten, and I prefer to hang mine on the wall. My father liked to play in the garden. He would nurture his plants and hedges and attack our lawn with a vengeance although it was quite clear that the war he waged against the dandelions and crabgrass was hopeless. Renewed after hours of playing in the dirt, he was able to return to his profession, playing with ideas in a big advertising firm. He has told me that his complete concentration on the garden left his unconscious mind free to gather ideas. Problems which had confounded him found solutions.

In order to have full access to our personal resources we need to have as complete an understanding as possible of who we are and what kind of balance has been struck within us or what kind of transactions are likely to be made by our inner congregation. This kind of self examination is a continual process. It requires enormous effort and certainly we can never say that we have come to the end of it.

We must ask ourselves what kind of inner child we have carried with us from childhood. Is our internal parent nurturing, responsive and caring, or angry, critical, and fearful, or perhaps a combination of the two? We need to understand how that parent has instructed us in the past in order to know how it works within us now. Does it encourage with approval and lead by example, or manipulate with guilt and intimidate with anger, or bribe with unrealistic or inappropriate rewards? Depending upon what we find in examining our inner parent history, we can proceed as adults to take control of the transactions between the inner child and the parent tape. Now, this sounds like a great game to me. Sometimes being in control will require that we ignore our parent tapes. How many times have your own kids, your own parent or your employees done that? Sometimes you just have to clearly point out to yourself and declare the inappropriateness of the rewards promised by the parent tape, i.e.: safety, fame, food or power. Your own adult self can transact a compromise of the very sort that accompanies good negotiations.

Here's an example. I say to myself, "Self, let's take a whole week and just hang out in the studio and make stuff." (Substitute sewing room, corner of the garage, or whatever spot you nest in.) Now, that's the kid wanting to come out and play. At this point the parent tape says, "You haven't got time for that," and then comes the inevitable list of reasons why such a commitment of time isn't possible: the kids, the house, the job, the aging parent, the neighbor, the spouse, and so on. Many of us will just hang our heads, kick the cat and accept the list. The inner child is, once more, relegated to the back of the bus and

30

there she sits with her desire to play, and no one to permit her to do so. Unless, and this is the key, unless the adult self takes over and validates the need to play and negotiates a compromise. Here is the transaction: "What if," says the adult, "we play for a day and meet the needs of the family at meal time, then take another day to do the list and another day of play in the studio? If we play and work and then play again, will you (speaking to the parent tape) back off and let us enjoy this creative time in peace?"

This kind of transaction must be done consciously, with enormous attention paid to those inner voices that will tug and pull. Without some kind of balance in life the child within, in a fit of temper, may choose to sulk, to become depressed. She might take off an entire month or a year, but that will bring her no joy for the parent tape will work her over every step of the way unless she comes to the right terms with it. In order to learn to be our whole selves most of us have to do reconstructive work, evening out the relationships within and giving the personality full voice.

This process occurs again and again, not just when we spend time, but when we spend money, how much and on what? When acquisitions are made, how many and where to put them? Whenever there is a transaction or a junction where the several aspects of one's personality struggle to gain control, a deal must be struck. Whether or not it is a healthy one depends on the mediation of our inner adult. If the child is still in charge the person will do unexpected and out of control things. If the parent tape is in charge, reactions may be rigid and authoritarian in the extreme or too cautious or self-effacing. But if a person's own adulthood takes command, she can have access to every aspect, every resource of herself. She can reach her full potential.

Now, for what it's worth, you have my permission to play.

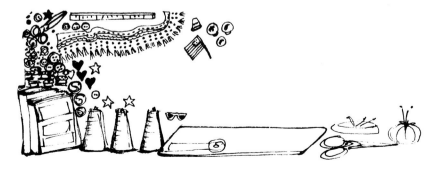

5.
A Space to Play In

So let's walk into our sewing room. I have called mine a studio, thus elevating it in the eyes of my family. I am indeed fortunate to have a room at all. I started with a small space behind our refrigerator. But at least it was a place where my machine could be left out continually.

Let's assume that you have been blessed with a space all your own. Look around. I hope you can see your materials, mountains of magic-colored fabrics. Color is indeed a wondrous world and the whole spectrum should await you in this room. Every red and combination thereof that can be found, every green and every yellow like sunlight dancing should fill the eye. When I look at such a display my response is that of an eager child. Combining colors and patterns has always been easy for me. Though it made my mother moan, I blended plaids and stripes, blues and greens like a Gypsy. There is permission all around to combine color in ways that create excitement. Consider the tiger lily, the pansy, or tiny forget-me-nots, and for me the adult world was fortuitously permitting. My Aunt Isabel O'Neil was an artist of the painted finish, and she had orange and fuchsia carpets which met at a doorway.

That junction shaped my life. I dreamed of a skirt of fuchsia and orange chiffon billowing about me. I even tried to make it. It was a disaster but some day, some day.

So in this studio the fabric is visibly available. If this is not possible then just like your three-year-old, you'll have to take it all out of its hiding place and sit in it. Every stimulation available needs to be touched and handled.

Not surprisingly, those of us who work in fabric become collectors of it. However, collecting for many may be a fertile field for parent tapes such as: "This is a frivolous expenditure," "a storage problem," "a needless acquisition," "you already have too much" and other guilt trips. This is particularly true when you collect in bags. This project and that, each in its own little sack, can not be seen or enjoyed. It is nothing but a constant reminder of dreams that have not yet come to fruition. If I had my way, no one would have bags of guilt accumulating at her feet. Dump it all out and give it meaning. A collection has an order and significance all its own.

Some of us do not have our own inner permission to collect anything for which there is not an immediate and pressing need. Under some circumstances, we do not have permission from others either. Spouses with boats, huge libraries, old cars and computers, can find our collections of fabric excessive. Of course, as people of the late twentieth century, we are less likely to take the "bull moose" approach to things too seriously; but I have students who see themselves as victims and they are only too willing to make sacrifices to please, to chase the approval they have never gotten and most surely never will receive as victims. These are often women who have been abused and you will know them by the fear that meets you in the air around them. I have had many of them in class and although I would gather them in my arms to comfort them and rail against those who have so thoughtlessly used them, these are women who cannot change without extensive professional help. The best we can do is to acknowledge their pain and encourage them.

Those of us who are fortunate enough to be dealing with only a small amount of manageable guilt can collect. We can ignore or compromise with our parent tape, stand up to our mates, laugh at our children, or in a pinch use subterfuge. We need to acquire a vocabulary of threads, embroidery floss, pearl cottons, crochet string, metallics . . . oh, the list goes on. Trims—don't you just love them?—fabrics, mechanical devices, scissors that you can be proud of, rotary cutters, anything that you need for creative play. Long ago I made out a check list that I feel will equip anyone who is taking a recreational sewing class. Here it is. You may find it useful.

- [ ] paper and pencil
- [ ] pins and pin cushion
- [ ] safety pins
- [ ] extra bobbins
- [ ] embroidery flosses
- [ ] vocabulary of threads
- [ ] scissors that cut
- [ ] paper scissors
- [ ] sewing machine and knowhow
- [ ] paper glue stick
- [ ] see-through plastic ruler
- [ ] tape measure
- [ ] rotary cutter
- [ ] cutting mat
- [ ] glue gun and glue
- [ ] name tags
- [ ] selection of marking pens
- [ ] crochet thread
- [ ] thimble
- [ ] Scotch tape

- [ ] a variety of hand-sewing needles: yarn darners, doll-making needles, 3½″ and 5″ embroidery needles, sharps and quilting needles

- [ ] stuffing tools: surgical clamp, Bow Whip turner, Chinese wok stick

- [ ] an apple for the teacher and a sense of humor

Let's go shopping. We can look through a mail-order catalog, a local quilt shop, a junk shop, thrift shop, full fabric store, your mother's closet, you name it. We walk in, listening to our inner child. What she loves she gets. If she needs limits, set them; but do not limit her with finger-wagging shoulds and shouldn'ts. Creating with an abundance of choices is enormously exciting. Most of all, remember end use does not need to be established for a thing to have value. To allow a thing to pass through your fingers like a handful of gold coins is enough; you have been allowed to love it, perhaps to envision it as part of something or as on it. Perhaps one day your thing will find itself in the hands of another collector to be loved again and seen anew. One should never hold things too dear, nor for too long. But for now hold it to the light, let the color and the image dance before you and take your pleasure in the moment of your seeing.

The collection that you and I are looking for makes sense to the way we work. It has a meaning of its own. It is a useful thing organized in a way that suits only ourselves. I have a friend who, in a fit of the guilts, hired someone to organize her workroom. It was a disaster. Everything was so neatly stored away with cute little labels that she was loathe to create any new disorder. Now there are many who cannot function without a high degree of order. To each his own. You must find what suits you best.

I have had several students ask me how much yardage or how many of one thing they should have in their collection. This is a good question and, as you might guess, a hard one to answer. As a dollmaker I usually think in terms of one yard cuts, but I break all of my own rules all the time. Sometimes I know I have to wear the stuff; needless to say, this requires a good deal more than one yard. There is, of course, the incredible piece you know you'll never see again or one that is so cheap that you get some for yourself and some to share. And then there are muslins or flesh colors that you buy by the bolt. Often your local quilt shop will give you a substantial discount when you order a whole bolt, or a case of stuffing. I think that the guiding question is: how can I make this collection work for me?

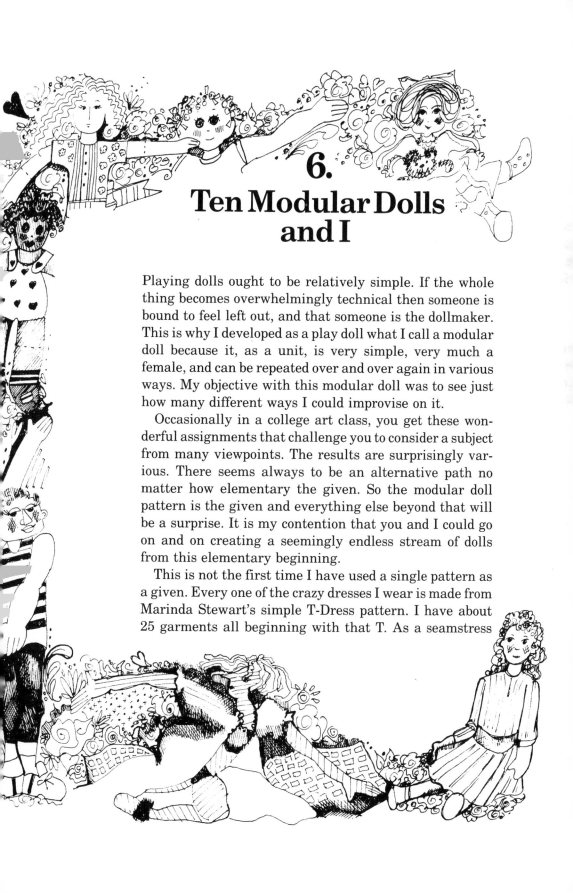

6.
Ten Modular Dolls
and I

Playing dolls ought to be relatively simple. If the whole thing becomes overwhelmingly technical then someone is bound to feel left out, and that someone is the dollmaker. This is why I developed as a play doll what I call a modular doll because it, as a unit, is very simple, very much a female, and can be repeated over and over again in various ways. My objective with this modular doll was to see just how many different ways I could improvise on it.

Occasionally in a college art class, you get these wonderful assignments that challenge you to consider a subject from many viewpoints. The results are surprisingly various. There seems always to be an alternative path no matter how elementary the given. So the modular doll pattern is the given and everything else beyond that will be a surprise. It is my contention that you and I could go on and on creating a seemingly endless stream of dolls from this elementary beginning.

This is not the first time I have used a single pattern as a given. Every one of the crazy dresses I wear is made from Marinda Stewart's simple T-Dress pattern. I have about 25 garments all beginning with that T. As a seamstress with only modest dressmaking skills, I have tried to avoid the biggest problem one finds in sewing for one's self: fitting. I have split it up the front to make a vest, a jacket, or a coat. And when I have to make one of those size ten garments for the big Fairfield–Concord Fashion Shows, I have "the revenge of the fat lady" and add a gusset so that I can wear the thing a year later after it has been on tour.

PAINTED LADY

So, for starters, I thought I would make this modular doll ten different ways. For those of you who wondered how I get from here to there, I will describe the process. First I took the doll's pattern and added 60 visual pounds to her. You can do this by adding a ¼" seam allowance. I wanted her to look a bit more like her mother. In addition, since I had decided to tatoo her entire body with fabric paint, having her larger gave me more body to paint—and I love to paint. I didn't want the painting to have any reference to reality. The audience would know what to expect if the tatoos were realistic and then where would I get the dismay, shock or surprise?

I selected muslin as a neutral surface although I could as well have selected a yellow or green fabric. Perhaps next time. I used Delta fabric dyes to do the painting. I apply them with either brush or the tube they came in. These dyes have a textile medium (sold with the dyes), that is brushed into the surface of the fabric or mixed with the dyes themselves. Remember these are dyes, so keep your sleeves out of them.

I could have used acrylic paint instead, but it would have

Painted Lady

required that I treat the surface with a gesso ground which would have made it stiff. What makes the dyes a pleasure to use is that they dry quickly. Patience has never been one of my virtues, and with the textile medium on the surface I can get a very expressive line.

The current craze for sweatshirt painting has encouraged paint companies to make some of their products three dimensional. Paints come both shiny and matte, with puffs and even glitter. They are applied with their own containers. The dye is so stiff that it holds small objects like plastic rhinestones and buttons. You can finish raw edges with it. Fun Fun Fun! In addition to fat paint there are metallics and glitter, and tints. Now, how can one resist playing in all that nonsense?

The painted surface is exciting because you can meander about, applying images as they occur in your head. No seams are necessary, and no piecing. Of course it helps if you have a little facility with a brush, but dots and dashes in wonderful colors will do as well. Gay abandon is essential and if something doesn't work to please you, you can cover it over with more paint. You can even glue fabric over an area that seems muddy.

With the skills of a child doing finger painting you can paint. You simply have to change your expectations to meet the level of your skills. Let's explore a parallel here. A child, your child, sits down to paint. You watch, anticipating the work of a child and praise her accordingly. Then you encourage her to stretch a bit. "Draw that tree over there," or "Tell me about that shape over there," giving her courage to explore her potential. Finally, you both stand back and admire. You, perhaps, are wise enough to congratulate yourself on how well you managed to facilitate this little learning experience.

You must teach yourself in the same way. First of all, base your expectations on reality. Patiently push yourself into unfamiliar territory. Impatience with your own inner child will only make her withdraw or give up. She will become agitated and convinced that she cannot do what you want. Remember that teaching yourself new skills is not unlike teaching a child. Use encouragement and reinforcement, and be your own cheerleader.

So, here is my first doll. Have you started yours? Meantime, here are more of my modular dolls together with their stories. . . .

BORN TO BE SUSAN

When the Flying Phoebes decided to use the modular doll as a step-by-step monthly workshop I selected an outrageously bright pink for the body. Before cutting I (again) added an extra ¼″ seam allowance around the pattern so that when she was sewn, she'd look as though she weighed 60 pounds more than the modular doll.

I inserted a profile nose at the side seam on the head so she could look over her shoulder and added some stuffed lip to make her a bit more sensuous. I had been given a nylon filament yarn by Foster Fiberlon which, when untwisted and scored with my fingernail, came out like the crimped hair popular in the 60s and now resurfacing on my 15-year-old Laura. I knotted the hair in the middle and frizzed it all over. I had selected red hair which was quite fetching with her bright pink body. And there she sat until her nakedness took the form of an accusation and I felt obliged to clothe her before the fall chill set in. (It was also time for the underwear meeting at doll club.)

At this point a peculiar thing happened. The Pink Lady began to look as if she wanted a pair of suede boots, so I yielded to her request and made them. Then she told me, ever so shyly, that she thought a pair of black lace panties would do to cover her; and she flatly refused a bra.

This inanimate creature was obviously becoming a person, one capable of making demands. As I looked at her for further direction, I discovered that she had become a student of mine who has taken several of my classes and from whom I had learned much. Susan is a psychologist and a teacher of sex education in a college near Fresno and we have hit it off well. Since this doll was obviously herself, I took a piece of silk chiffon from the thirties that she had given me. She had said when she did it that she thought it must belong to me as it no longer belonged to her. The doll loved the blouse, and then began eying a piece of East Indian embroidery for a vest and a brooch and earrings to complete the picture. Short of her glasses she was complete.

SIMPERING SWEETNESS

I call this doll Simpering Sweetness. As you have probably guessed, I am not a cute specialist. Most of the dolls that I have made would not be thought of as cute, but I hated to think that I lacked the ability, so I challenged myself the cute to see if I could do it. This time I had to make a trip to one of my local quilt shops where I knew I could find a generous supply of extra sweet fabric. I selected the pieces that I thought would be indisputably darling and

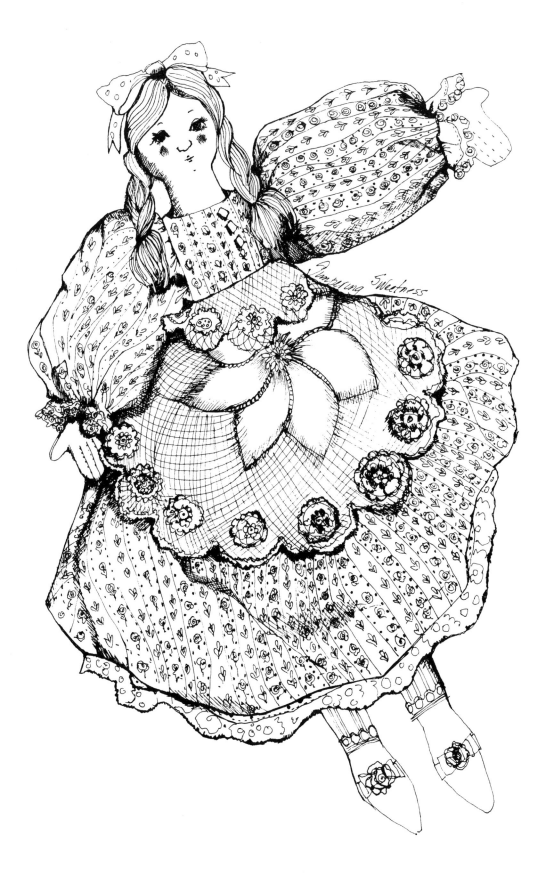

bought a yard of everything. The gals at the shop who knew me could not resist the impulse to ask why this sudden interest in pretty, sweet, cute and dear. I just giggled and left.

One thing about "doing" cute that should be noted here is that it can be addictive. It was very easy for me to create this cute doll and most people loved her except for my not-so-cute friends who turned sarcastic at the sight of her. Because I enjoyed doing it, I feel I should sound a warning. If you ever think of yourself as being on the road to profound, remember that there's this side street marked Simpering Sweetness. Beware.

Miss Simpering has petticoats, lace stockings, bow lips, and lots and lots of buttons and bows. She is blond and blue eyed and everything that I am decidedly not.

EVE AND I

Eve, for this is her name, began as a challenge in stitchery and buttons. Then as I began to think of her, I added a philosophical dimension, something that had been rolling around in my head for some time and needed expressing.

It seems to me that we are all limited. I am not all that you are and you are not all that I am. It is my belief that no one can possess talent, that we are all merely conduits through which creativity may flow if we permit. Every gift of talent belongs to the collective whole and individuals are merely stewards. It behooves us, if we hope to have access to this flow of creativity, to value and care for those who possess in their stewardship that which we do not have. So the richest among us is the person whose love includes all people, and the poorest is the one who cuts himself off from others with bigotry and fear. So I stitched myself in Eve, being born of her and her difference, thus extending myself beyond what I am. And I try always to ask of every soul who enters my life, "Bring me your diversity and let me learn through your eyes to see the world as you can see it."

Philosophy aside, I used the pattern as a template and drew around it so that I could work on the fabric before the doll was stuffed. I changed the head to make it a bit rounder and the hands to make them larger. When I came

Eve and I

to the embroidery on the back of the body, I stitched up the doll first because I found that I was doing wasted work over the edge and feared that if I stretched the piece during stuffing, everything would be out of whack. I then completed the stitching on a stretched surface, using a single small stitch to anchor the thread whenever I sewed into the body. I made my stitches wherever I felt like. I call this approach stream of consciousness. Whatever occurs to you to do, do it; don't worry about any nagging from a critic. If you take this approach enough, you begin to trust that little girl inside.

I finally added some buttons on Eve and made a simple tee coat which is like a Japanese field jacket. Some of the images that I stitched on Eve's body and the jacket had meaning in the context of the statement I was trying to make. The vines symbolize the green and growing things of the earth. The eye is the intuitive self which I feel Africans are so much closer to than I. The fish signifies the life force, and you can see me waiting to be born.

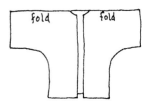

THE QUEEN OF HEARTS

"Modify that pattern," I said to myself, and my mind went over and over all the changes that I could possibly imagine. Enlarge the head, cut it off. Lengthen the legs, tie them in knots. Make the arms go around me; do I have enough material for that?

Finally it became apparent that I had to go to paper and disgorge myself of all these ideas that were keeping me up nights and driving me crazy during the day.

So I added fingers to the hands and lengthened the legs, exaggerated the feet and enlarged the head . . . and there she was! I applied orange hair to her yellow-striped body (New Year's resolution: no more flesh colored dolls). I keyed up the colors for the dress using only geometric print to give her rhythm. I tried my hand at machine-embroidering the face to good effect. When I followed the hair line in stitching the eyes, she did, however, insist on assuming a harassed and worried expression. "Oh dear!" she said, trying to move her two fingers so they would meet in space, "Am I quite mad?"

Right within reach of the glue gun was a neat little

46

Queen of Hearts........

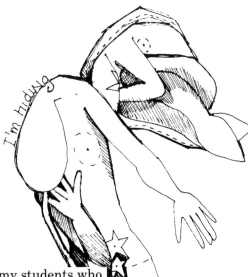

finger pin cushion given to me by one of my students who thought I could use some order in my life. So I snapped off the elastic that went around your finger and made the pin cushion into a ring and hot-glued it right on top of her head and she became the Queen of Hearts reacting to the theft of her tarts. Have you ever, in all your life, gotten a satisfactory answer to the perennial question, "Who did that?"

I'M HIDING

I had written on my list of things to do: "Make a modular doll in the fetal position." You know, the position you crawl into when too many demands and too little time drive you to your bed. There you wind up, sucking your thumb and rocking.

As I conceived of the form this doll would take, I found myself thinking of the birth of my first child. "She's a Navajo," said my mother. "She's purple." And she was. Evalyn, destined to have a stunning dark complexion, was purple indeed.

So I found cloth in an appropriate shade, and used the finger design from the Queen of Hearts. I stitched a long umbilical cord to wrap her in and anchored it in the seam at the top of her head, and stuck one of her fingers into her mouth. I used star sequins for eyes, covered her nakedness with more stars and stuffed her lightly to make her pliable. I locked her other arm in place so her knees could be drawn up, then rolled her into a ball and took a long look, and envied her.

48

MAN AND WOMAN

From the perspective of a modern female looking at this old world for some sign that it understands how wasted women have been, how used and abused, victimized and trivialized, it is not easy to be generous in including men, on any level, in the future. I mean, do we need this?

However, considering that many men seem inclined to agree with this dim view of their own sex, one cannot help noticing that, with the exception of the human race, all other living things seem to have struck some kind of balance. So even though I see women as having more endurance than men, more intuition, more compassion and more general usefulness, I have come to believe that they were placed on this earth for a purpose. And if we are to continue to evolve, then we must conceive of a balance, and a joining . . . hence these dolls called Man and Woman.

Each different but joined as the dolls are, could we men and women of today not see in our differences our greatest mutual advantage and borrow from one another's strengths, mutually consenting to allow the other to exist with dignity? Why not?

Springing as we do from common dust, my dear
Your dust or mine?
Rib of your rib or
Soul of my soul?
The we one flesh or twain?
Enemies or friends?
That, I think, is the game.

WOMAN

MAN

AN ANGEL

The making of an angel brings to mind a consideration of
flight, and although I doubt that angels have any need for
wings I sympathize with the artist who first conceived of
angels being thus equipped because wings have such aes-
thetic appeal. Recently I got hold of a product called "Creative Twist." It is made from paper, usually something
like a paper bag, and then twisted. It comes in long strips
which you untwist and make into all sorts of things. The
company sent me some that was made out of cellophane.
It hits the light and takes on the colorations of an oil slick.
I couldn't wait to try this out as wings.

Old lace seemed naturally fit for angels, and old buttons
and ribbon. Linen handkerchiefs and stitchery to blend it
all. Then came the hair. Yarn seemed to overwhelm this
fantasy of flight so I found some old wool in my collection
of things too good to throw away. Which, by the way, I
had had for more than two years. I say this to dispel any
"use it or lose it" nonsense. The doll loved the hair which
softly displayed itself in front of the wings as she prepared
to take flight.

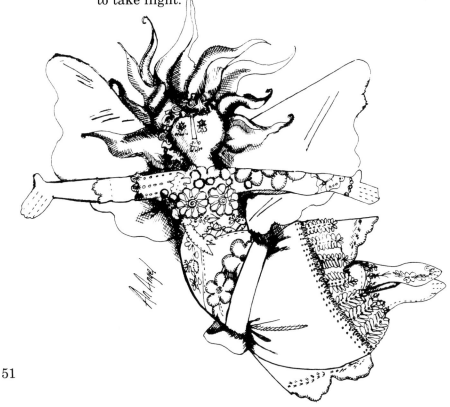

IT'S NOT YOUR TIME YET

I remember how it feels to be buried in children, putting off me for them. When I was wise I did it willingly and when I was foolish I did it kicking and screaming as if the volume of my screams would change my circumstance or theirs. Now they are not young and I have time to construct a world of my own. What we have learned in each other's arms I cannot put a price on, and the pleasure that they give me cannot be expressed. I will never stitch a master-piece I think, but these souls with whom I have nested have taught me not to care. I cannot see them in each other's company without understanding that it is they who are the masterpieces and I did but stand and wait.

So the colors of these dolls are bright and full. The mother figure embraces and is embraced. The children nourish and are nourished. But for the time they are over-whelming, and there are surely moments when one sees no hope of emerging from motherhood with even a shred of identity in tact. It is very much like yielding to a great wave, a kind of death.

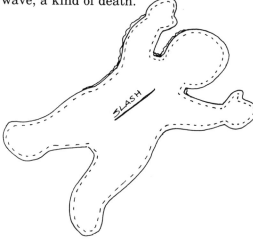

Trinkets, such as the watch and key chain that have been included in this piece, are the kind you collect over time until the moment when they become "just the thing." The freedom to use them came from having had them long enough not to feel the loss too greatly. The babies were stitched all around and then an opening was cut in the front to turn them inside out. Since they face the mother doll you don't see the opening. The batting was stitched into the seam. They were then stitched to the mother doll.

PRETTY & PUNK

When I began this project I made a list of projects which I duly cast in cement. Once they were written down, I was going to do them. No cheating. Of all the assignments this is the one I was least interested in. I am not a party girl. I feel uncomfortable with a group of people who are trying too hard to have fun. I'd rather be at home sewing. So I decided that the person who was going to this party was definitely not me. I was sending her and I would make her clothes but I definitely was not going to this party.

The advantage that occurs in making dolls who are going to a party is that you don't have to have yards and yards of expensive exotic fabric to drape them in. They will make do with bits and pieces of things that you have (have been forced to keep because they were too wonderful to throw away). The real party spirit is in the masked ball, so why not a gold lamé face and feather hair, lace tights and a "drop-dead gorgeous" coat which I could never afford myself. Off she goes, well equipped to be master of her fate. She'll know all the right things to say and have the panache to pull it off.

54

7.
A Day in Class
With the Modular Doll

When women sign up to play for a day and put themselves into the somewhat uncomfortable position of not knowing what is expected of them, they are probably what I call stretchers. Stretchers are people who exercise their brains, going beyond the comfortable into the uncomfortable, where all the growing takes place.

The class that I designed around the modular doll was intended to tempt the timid to stretch too. Since this simple doll presents no technical problems they could be encouraged to make changes easily, modifying the pattern if they chose. The doll is an adult female so they could play with their own body awareness. They could make fun of their body or idealize it; that would be their choice.

The first Play Day I held was offered in a shop in Berkeley called New Pieces. Eight brave souls, in an appropriately flexible state of mind, marched into class with their doll bodies already in hand. One mother signed up with her two children, a boy eight and a girl eleven. She was their facilitator and did what they wished done to their dolls, and the dolls became respectively male and female. The boy insisted that if his sister's doll had breasts his should be fully equipped as well. Two beads and a loop of cloth would do. The girl's doll was black with one turquoise leg and one fuchsia. The other women had dolls of bright pink, stripes and white flowers. Some were simply in muslin. One of the dollmakers had made hers with significant erotic overtones, but this was indeed Berkeley, the land of the free, so I took a deep breath and plunged in.

First came the face. I had prepared for the class by collecting as much "kitsch" as I could find in order to stimulate the students: paint and sequins, buttons and a multitude of nonsense. I showed the class how the placement of the face could change the appearance. Several students chose to applique on a folded nose. Some used beads and sequins, some simply drew in the features with a fine tip permanent marking pen.

One student, to be on the safe side, felt the need to draw her face with a water removable pen that she could erase. Hers was the face of an old lady who was a composite of several people in her life including herself. Her doll was to have the "appearance of wisdom," she said. But she was a woman of questionable taste. The doll wore an oddment of clothing reminiscent of the thirties and trimmed in old lace. She made her a jacket of an old silk panel with a Japanese girl on it. The doll emerged as an undeniably romantic soul.

It was interesting to find another person charmed by what we both designated as a Little Old Lady, genteel secret keeper of the wisdom of the child. One student painted her face and added shiny cellophane eyes.

The most delightfully outrageous face started with bubble gum. The doll was blowing a huge face-engulfing bubble. The mouth was made of two back-to-back buttons. The bubble was of bright pink cloth, cut in circles and stuffed. I loved that doll most I think.

The next step was hair. Hair can appear as a mass or as sculpture. It can be applied as cloth, paint or stitchery. One can make it—to mention a few ideas—with torn fabric, strings, yarns, metallic threads, wires, or oven-baked curls (acrylic yarn wrapped around a metal knitting needle and cooked for 20 minutes). How about snaps or buttons, or beads, cloves, cinnamon sticks, bows or ball fringe, fur or postage stamps? Anything you can think you can do.

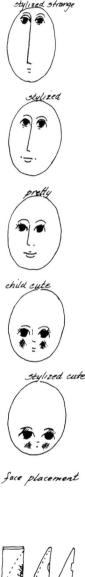

stylized strange

stylized

pretty

child cute

stylized cute

face placement

Applied Nose . . .

56

Bubble Gum Doll

The class looked at everything that had been gathered. The two children tried several things and the girl settled on a huge pipe cleaner for her black doll. The boy used bits of yarn. For some reason he had now decided that his doll would be a tourist. Perhaps in that sea of women that's what he felt like. He began to look for gaudy tropical prints for a shirt and shorts. The two fairy dolls were wigged with an abundance of exotic yarns, flowers, wires and assorted spangles. The Little Old Lady had her orange yarn hair marceled. The bubble gum kid had red feathers and turquoise yarn and was beginning to look decidedly like Cindy Lauper, the rock star. Another doll who had antique buttons for eyes and looked a little fierce had a slightly frazzled doll wig. With all that hair she became a bit less frightening. The bright pink punk doll required two pieces of fake fur in chartreuse and fuchsia sewn together at the part. By this time the entire class was giggling.

Play and laughter protect the mind from fear of failure. We may fear looking ridiculous but when the whole group is being silly it's hard to think of yourself as the only one who is a little off. Since the entire class was out of control we all entered in. We gave each other permission.

The possibilities for clothing the dolls were many. After all, anything that comes in a sheet form, from paper to cloth, or tin to plastic, can make clothes. First came the underwear and everyone got exotic. Black lace, white lace and flower patches hidden by a gee string. It was clear that these women had a statement to make about their own sexuality and that they felt safe in making it here.

Finally the outer clothes. The bubble gum girl had a silver lamé knit top with a gold polka dot net skirt. The punk doll had leather underwear, purple boots and a skirt patterned with skulls and flames. We might call that playing with something we're afraid our children might become or we're sorry we missed. The children, with the help of their mother, finished the gaudy tourist and an exotic black woman in a gold lamé jumpsuit. The two fairies had donned translucent wings and an abundance of flowers. That overdressed doll with the wig was now ready for a party or the opera with polka dot netting all over her body and wonderful sandals with heels made of gold thimbles. Lastly the Little Old Lady trotted out wearing a soft green dress with beige lace, her coat as yet unmade.

The class deepened our concept of female play, which we

could take home and use in our own surroundings. It was a real experiment and a distinct success.

There have since been other classes. The Flying Phoebes tried it, the Columbia Stitchers, The Quilt Gallery in Kallispell, Montana, and the doll club at Tayo's in Fair Oaks, California. Three of the dolls created in these groups are pictured in the foldout. Bliss, My Twisted Sister was done by Elaine Spence of Portland, Oregon, an exuberant creature who suffers from the same crippling arthritis that her maker does. A Blue Denim Beauty came from Anne Brasher of Sacramento, and an exhausted, tortured Fitness Fanatic, from Bobbi Lachenmyer of the Phoebes.

This is what we've done so far, and now it's your turn. The pattern is at the end of the book for you to use. You have your collection and your imagination. Get a group together and let's play dolls.

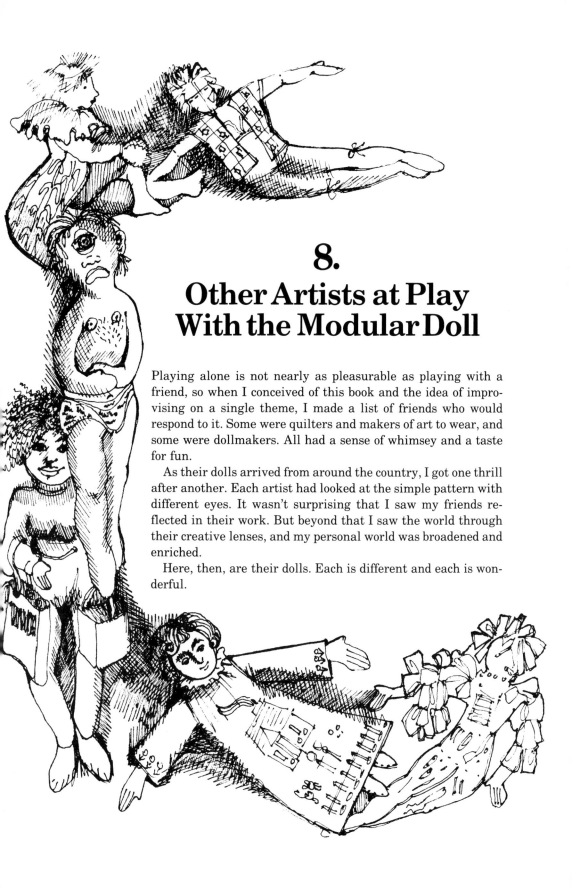

8.
Other Artists at Play With the Modular Doll

Playing alone is not nearly as pleasurable as playing with a friend, so when I conceived of this book and the idea of improvising on a single theme, I made a list of friends who would respond to it. Some were quilters and makers of art to wear, and some were dollmakers. All had a sense of whimsey and a taste for fun.

As their dolls arrived from around the country, I got one thrill after another. Each artist had looked at the simple pattern with different eyes. It wasn't surprising that I saw my friends reflected in their work. But beyond that I saw the world through their creative lenses, and my personal world was broadened and enriched.

Here, then, are their dolls. Each is different and each is wonderful.

CURTIS GRACE

Some things are worth waiting for, such as Valentina. When the box arrived with her inside, I was so delighted to see her, I simply didn't mind that she was slightly over deadline. Included with her was a letter, written significantly by hand, explaining why Curtis had found it impossible to do this project in the one day that I had assigned to it.

"Please allow me to share my feelings regarding playtime. As you know, I prefer to handsew rather than work by machine. Right then and there I threw out the idea of a one-day doll. I made her out of things that I had on hand. I used things that would make the doll easy to assemble. The shirt I cut from an old hankie. The coins and the bells found in her jewelry had been earmarked for a jacket that I am working on, but Valentina insisted. There is a point for me when I am making dolls that the character of the doll gains the upper hand and I have no control over the outcome. While I tried not to spend a lot of time creating her, Valentina had an opposing view and would not let me put her down until she felt that she was finished.

"In regard to playtime, I am fortunate enough to be self employed and I make my living decorating for large parties and creating window displays for retail shops (dressing big dolls). I couldn't have imagined a better answer to the query, 'What are you going to do when you grow up?' than what I am doing.

"In addition to making dolls I collect toys, dolls and children's books. I have been a serious collector since I was twelve. Playtime, to me, has always been the time that I spent in collecting things and making things from my collections. In fact, the artistic process is my idea of play. As a child, once I had my books cut out or my cardboard houses finished, I spent very little time playing with them. I was ready to create something else."

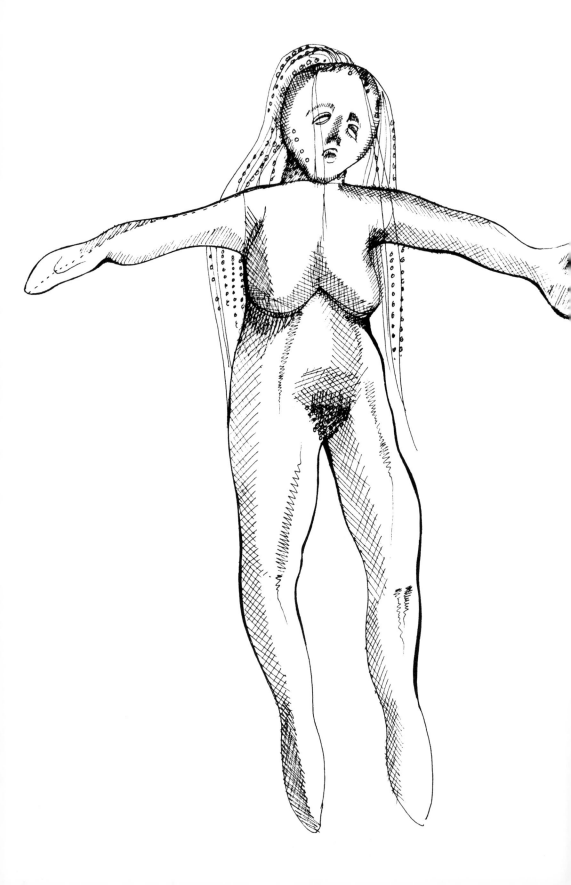

SUSANNA OROYAN

Since 1982 Susanna Oroyan has been a member of The National Association of American Doll Artists, a most prestigious group which can only be joined by invitation. She is now its president and in her second term. She holds the record for being the most experimental dollmaker in the group. She is forever trying something new which is no doubt the reason she and I became friends over the telephone. We have found endless things to talk about, as our phone bills attest. Susanna did not hesitate a moment in accepting my invitation to play with the modular doll and promised me that I would be surprised, maybe even shocked with the results. I was. You may have noticed that those of us who have been designated by our peers as being at the fringe come to take a kind of pride in the designation.

Susanna says that she has no problem with ideas. Her 18-foot table is littered with partially completed projects. "I have a problem convincing myself that they have not been done because I thought of them." Regardless of this lifetime supply of unfinished symphonies, Susie marches on to complete enough work to keep us in awe.

Her organizational skills and her mastery of words served her well in writing the book *A Collector's Guide to Contemporary Artist Dolls* with Carol-Lynn Russell Waugh and doing a regular column for the *Doll Reader*. All this tells us that she is a doer as well as well as a dreamer.

For Susie play can be a group effort. She and several friends in Eugene, Oregon are continually playing with dolls. She told me of one very involved play which included adopting a forlorn and tawdry French bed doll and trying, without success, to reform her. She would just reach a state of repentance when the good life would prove too much for her and she would be forced to run back to life on the streets. Heaven only knows what she was up to. Days later she would come back looking worse than ever begging for a bed, only to re-group and run off again to the bars. This hilarity would run its course and another play would begin. We are never too old, friends; we are never too old.

The gold lamé Mom Goddess was definitely a surprise. Her mask is of Sculpy which is a resin clay, and she makes a haunting display.

BARBARA CHAPMAN: Interview follows foldout on page 65

ELINOR PEACE BAILEY:
Angel

CURTIS GRACE:
Valentina

ELAINE SPENCE:
Bliss, My Twisted Sister

SUSANNA OROYAN:
Mom Godess

BARBARA CHAPMAN

I walked into a yarn store in Encinitas, California a few years ago, not because I was taken up with knitting but because I was taken in by the colors of the yarn. The lighting was dim and as I looked about my eyes gravitated to a glorious rendition of The Three Kings standing above me on the shelf.

"Whose dolls are those?" I shouted. "Oh, those belong to Barbara Chapman," said the shop owner. I held my breath hoping that she would give me the information that would put me in touch with this incredible lady. Fortunately she didn't hesitate for a moment, and I was able to set up a meeting with Barbara. Nothing could have prepared me for the exotic world I entered when I was welcomed into her home. Never had I seen such wonders. Not only were her dolls encrusted with findings of ethnic handwork from all over the world, but every surface in her home was also encrusted. I was transfixed as she showed me her crocheted garments appliqued all over with beading. Predictably it was her dolls in this incredible environment that excited me most.

In the 1950s the film biography of Vincent Van Gogh, *Lust for Life*, changed my life. It made me decide that I wanted to become an artist. This film had influenced Barbara as well. As a young married woman she had decided it was pointless to pursue making art because she felt that she could not draw. However, once she saw how Vincent Van Gogh had struggled all his life, she concluded that she could do no less than try. She felt invited to participate, to use what she perceived as her limited gifts to create beauty. And that she has done.

In ethnic museums, she finds herself hyper-ventilating, getting excited by ancient handwork from India, Africa and the Near East. The mystery of the layer upon layer of networking threads and beads compels her to join the dance, seeking images in the dust. A doll made by Barbara Chapman is a link with an ancient mind.

65

Continued from page 64

JEAN RAY LAURY

Jean Ray Laury is author of *Ho For California: Pioneer Women and their Quilts, Creative Women: Getting It All Together,* and *The Sunbonnet Sue Series.* Her contribution to the world of quilts and dolls is legendary. Her vision in the 60s, which validated decorative stitchery in clothing, and her love of whimsy which gave us her book, *The Creative Approach to Doll Making* (now out of print but well worth searching for) has opened many an eye to the artistic potential in the handwork of women.

The humor in her quilts warms the coldest of hearts. Jean tells of an occasion when her work was criticized for being too decorative. She gave the criticism some deep thought and then decided deliberately to explore to the nth degree her inclinations toward embellishment. Her tribute to her critic became *Fantasies of a Housewife,* a wonderful spoof on herself and all of us who take ourselves too seriously. Of all the artists represented in this book, Jean Ray Laury understands the value of play the best. Though her work is full of play, her design concepts are serious indeed. I was not the least surprised when I received her delightful felt doll. Who else but Jean Ray could give us ball fringe and make us like it?

The note that accompanied the doll told of the conflict the pattern had created in her. She felt the need of a poem to express it but had been unable to find the right words. It is unlikely that these words are right but . . .

A dollmaker known as Jean Ray
Had something important to say.
She tried to use boobs
But the boobs were refused.
So Goodie Two Shoes
Had it her way.

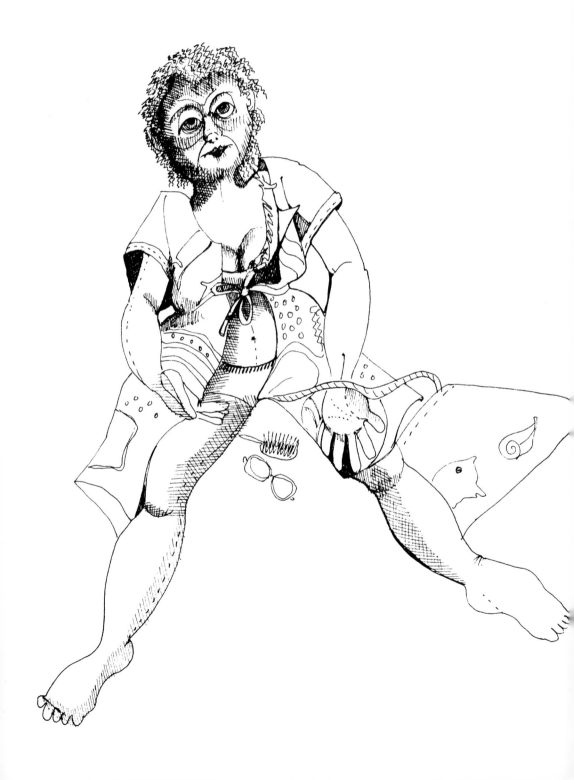

MARY BARTROP

She's learning how to juggle. It helps with her concentration, she says, and clears her mind. For the creative mind this clearing of the mind comes at a premium. I often think that my head looks like my studio, and that's frightening.

Mary says that she was born a dollmaker. She began by taking dolls apart and altering them. This caused a good deal of dissension between her and her sister because it was the sister's dolls whose hair was cut and dyed and her sister's dolls who were subjected to the various research projects that opened their innards to scientific study.

Mary makes dolls out of everything. Recently her father sent her some of her early efforts which he had discovered in a delicate state. Here were a myriad of tiny souls made out of clay that was rapidly deteriorating.

When adolescence arrived with all its inhibitions that told her she was too old to play with dolls, Mary made doll clothes for her cousins. Doll images persisted in her mind at college when she majored in elementary education with an art emphasis. She was encouraged by one of her professors for whom she did a self-revelatory portrait. The teacher saw the artist inside the student and welcomed her out in the open.

Mary still finds her confidence wanes in a class room setting. When she takes a class she first ascertains what everybody else is doing and then takes off in a different direction so as not to be compared and found wanting.

Mary's sunbaked version of the modular doll is in remembrance of a class we shared once. I was the teacher at the time and all excited by the Florida "kitsch" that surrounded us.

So this lady of the beach has her supply of "geegaws and gimcracks." Mary made her red as a lobster, and not exactly youthful. She'll suffer tomorrow but for today, "Let me get my rays."

CARYL BRYER FALLERT

The harried hostess with flaming red hair is definitely Caryl. She is not always harried, but like all of us who lead complicated and demanding lives she has times when she feels pulled in a multitude of directions. These are the times when self definition demands attention. Who are we and who's running our lives, if you please?

Caryl is an extraordinary quilter who has received widespread recognition for her wonderful quilts. It is obvious that her sewing machine is growing out of her arm and is as much a part of her as her beautiful red hair. So deftly does she use it that one of her quilts won a purchase award of ten thousand dollars from the American Quilter's Society in Kentucky. An incredible sum and a validation of machine piecing and quilting from a most prestigious show!

Caryl has been making art and sewing for years. She has a degree with a minor in art from Wheaton College and has studied art all over the midwest. Her sewing and her art became one when she discovered quilting. "I used to spread oatmeal and nylon stocking on my canvases," she says. "I love texture." Quilting fabric embraced all that excited her, and she could tote it about on the frequent flights she makes as a stewardess for United Air Lines. It is apparent from Caryl's Self Portrait that even on a more intimate surface her machine work has vigor and vitality. Notice that the face of the doll is done by machine.

When I received the doll in the mail and Caryl and I had a moment to talk, it was apparent that the doll had become a way to give substance to inner feelings of Caryl's. As with many who make dolls, the language of the act turns on the maker and speaks of her deepest self and its need to be nourished and healed.

SALLY LAMPI

Since Sally Lampi is not only my business partner and dear friend, but also lives up the street from me, she is, from time to time, called upon to jump up and down and show rapt enthusiasm for a new creation of mine. And since I too have been called into similar service on her behalf, we often see each other's works in progress. Between us we have witnessed a lot of artistic creation from conception to birth, and conversations about how it all happens occur naturally from time to time.

When I asked Sally to tell me how the creative process begins for her, she said, without hesitation, "Oh, I see something. . . ." "Cracks in the ceiling?" "No, people . . . kids, I see a child and that child has to become a doll." So Sally fiddles with that body, or that hair or, in some cases, those feet, until some little tyke sees the light of day, smirking, sulking or giving the world one last chance.

As a matter of fact Sally has designed several patterns that have begun with feet. I have accused her of having a foot fetish. "Not surprising," says she, as she points out her own feet which are not at all shy and delicate. This leads me to wonder if my own preoccupation with large hips could be explained in the same way.

With a large family Sally has had a need to develop her sense of humor. Life, she finds, does not come out neatly tied in bows. Humor for her has been what it has been for many of us, a sort of armor that allows us to meet the world with the courage it demands. Sally's line of doll patterns are like the real people in her life. She plays with their images in her head until they irritate her; then she lets them out.

LISA LICHTENFELS

In my talk with Lisa Lichtenfels I am climbing new heights, for she is the dollmaker's dollmaker. She is a woman who, like myself, eats, sleeps and drinks dolls. She told me that when I first explained my concern for the female re-connecting with her inner child she was concerned. Her own childhood, she said, had been one she would never wish to return to. Not an unfamiliar story among the women I know.

She had, however, spoken about the matter with her husband who is a poet. He had agreed that the seat of the creative soul was indeed the inner child and that she, unlike many, had managed to keep her child very much alive. So she came to separate the child from childhood.

Her next concern was her awareness that for her there are two significant parts to making art: conceptualization followed by the realization. Although the conceptualization is a grand forum for play, the realization of the concept requires a great deal of discipline and an enormous amount of work and is not, by her measure, play but work. Knowing, as I do, what is required to work as hard as Lisa does, I am certain that she is correct. We agreed that a piece that has not been in the conceptual or play stage long enough will turn out stale and simply technical.

Lisa told me that when she was a child she was only happy when she was alone and drawing or dreaming. These became one and same from time to time as her facility improved. As she thought she drew, and the two became one act. She ceased to be conscious of the pencil; it simply drew.

The necessity of making a living demands that all of us do for money what we would not do for love. But, as Lisa said, "You do one for the piper and then you must do one for your muse or whatever god you acknowledge." I agree, for the one gives life to the other.

VIRGINIA AVERY

Being alive takes on new meaning when you are speaking with Virginia Avery. Not withstanding her considerable reputation as the author of three books which include *Quilts To Wear*, published by Scribners, she is always ready to foster and cultivate in others the gifts that they have been given. I know this from personal experience. A generosity of soul seems always to be accompanied by a grand sense of humor. Jinny's wonderful garments crackle with wit as does she. It is always a delight to glimpse her with her ever present entourage, flying here and there in one of her stunning creations that she gives titles to such as "Don't Shoot the Piano Player, She's Doing the Best That She Can."

In addition to her quilting and teaching, Jinny and her King Street Stompers, a Dixie Land Jazz band of ten men led by herself, spend Sundays playing up a storm all over New York City. It is therefore hardly surprising that Lou-lou, Jinny's modular doll, fresh from the Left Bank in Paris, has come to take the New York jazz clubs by storm.

While opening up the box in which she arrived, I found a note which read: "My name is Lou-lou *de la mais oui*, and I am Jinny Avery's alter ego. I love to dress up; I love to have happy times. I sing . . . I have a very throaty, sexy voice and people love to have me sing ballads. I can belt out a real low down blues . . . I love parties and music and I also love to eat. Sometimes it's not the food so much as it is the people and the wonderful conversation and the friendships that go along . . . So here I am dying to see what my sisters look like and what kind of personalities they have."

I couldn't resist making a telephone call to announce that she had arrived in grand style. Jinny didn't answer, so in Lou-lou's French accent, I left a message on the tape telling her alter ego that people in California found her absolutely charming.

Jinny and I were playing dolls.

GLORIA WINER

Gloria knows more about who does what to whom than any other person I know. From her home in New Jersey she networks, by phone, by letter and through her publication, *Let's Talk Doll Making*. She communicates with dollmakers all over the world and then she delights in putting them together and watching what happens. Gloria has been working to found the Society of Professional Doll Makers to help artists make a living at making dolls. In fact the list of organizations in which she has an interest is as long as your arm. She has worked tirelessly to see it all come together. That is, of course, how she and I met.

In addition to being a communications expert, she is also a very able dollmaker. She has focused on cloth dolls made from knits and she manages her material very well, thank you. When I traveled east to give a class sponsored by the S.P.D., I introduced her to the wonders of woven fabric and color. On the basis of that experience, she was willing to take a risk on the modular doll, and she got hilarious results.

Gloria says, and I believe her, that she gets excited about nearly everything that she can see. In the case of this doll she got carried away by net stockings and high heels. Having no red feathers she made the cloak. "It was fun," she said. "I knew I was going to make a floozy, so I collected wild things and plunged right in." Plunging in is the essence of this lady. Jim, her husband, named the doll In Search Of The Wolf.

TRACY STILWELL

It was love at first sight when I saw Tracy Stilwell's dolls. They were hanging in a small gallery in Berkeley called New Pieces, which is also a quilt shop. I begged her phone number and called her immediately to get some slides to add to a growing collection I have been making. We had a long talk and Tracy told me about her effort to create a doll with each garment and quilt that she makes, an idea that I had been using as well, except that I started with the doll and then designed a garment and a quilt using the doll image as a two-dimensional motif.

Since this conversation Tracy has participated in the first Doll Maker's Magic Exhibit, a competition sponsored by V.I.P., a fabric manufacturer, and Fairfield Processing, makers of stuffing, which was held at one of the annual Quilt Markets in Houston, Texas. She took first prize. This kind of experience can only encourage her.

Tracy majored in Women's Studies and did her graduate work in Women's History at Sarah Lawrence College. She learned to sew from her mother, so it is not surprising that her need for self expression took her first to quilting, a woman's art form, then to garments and finally to dolls.

Fifteen years ago Tracy became dependent on drugs. When she faced the problem and began to heal herself, she used her dolls as a form of self-nurturing. This is not a new idea. It is being used by many therapists to reach and comfort the inner child. For more than five years Tracy has been "clean and sober," as they say. No small achievement.

Maxine, like many of the dolls in this collection, took on a life of her own, and started giving orders. Tracy wrote: "She is rather wild. As she was being developed we marveled at her breasts and I just couldn't cover them up. Then a mystery arose about the rest of her wardrobe and I made my first G-string. I have flashes of feeling guilty because she doesn't have more elaborate clothing, but I just listened to Maxine and she said she doesn't want any more." What's a mother to do?

COLLETTE WOLF

When we spoke about play and how to go about it, Collette Wolf, who publishes *Platypus Designs*, told me that her game nearly always begins with "What would happen if?" and she's off. "You have to be a risk taker," she said, "and shut off that automatic critic." All this sounded most familiar. She continued: "The women I teach don't seem to be too good at this. The mere mention of the words "create or design" seem to frighten them. I have to use substitutes like devise or prepare."

Since her experience seemed to be much the same as my own, I asked about her own childhood and how she had apparently won permission to play and create. She told me that her parents were performers. They were singers and Collette was born on one of their road trips. So it was no shock to her parents when Collette began making things out of what ever was about. She has always had permission to play.

As a teacher (and she is an excellent one), Collette has sought to open her students to the possibility of making their own creations. "Play is therapy," she says. "Creating something is the very best kind of medicine. It automatically makes you feel happy." See now, didn't I tell you?

It should be noted here that Collette's play with the modular doll was a bit more involved than she had initially planned, and you will note that the doll looks quite different from the original pattern. This is a perfectionist lady and anything she sets her hand to must represent her fine sense of craftsmanship. That always demands more. She was relieved when she finished the doll. It had been more of a project for her than either of us had planned. Shall we then note that some people take their play very seriously indeed and that perhaps Collette Wolf might be called a little bit compulsive. Also that she produced a perfect piece of work.

MIRIAM GOURLEY

The thing that draws you immediately to Miriam is her loveliness. Her speech and her manner and the color of her skin are strikingly from another age, one less touched by the rushing winds of change, an age somehow more graceful. The dolls and the garments that she designs reflect a simplicity and purity, and her color sense leads her down quiet paths less dramatic and combative than my own.

I asked Miriam about her childhood play and where it took her, and she told me about her passion for boxes which she turned into unpeopled rooms. She cut the furnishings from magazines and kept them about her until she tired of them and then went on to design new spaces, new worlds.

Her family had few resources, but Barbie dolls were important playthings for her and her sister. The two of them costumed their dolls elaborately. At one time there was a boy doll on the market which had been designed as a boyfriend for Midge. Her parents could not afford the doll so Miriam set out to make one for her sister with wire and clay. "It turned out quite well," she said.

Nothing is a greater challenge for an artistic person than trying to make art and raise a family or put one's spouse through school. Miriam is doing all. As her husband attends the Brigham Young University and juggles jobs, she manages three little ones and keeps her pattern-making business going. "I have given up keeping my home in order but the environment in which I work is very important. I have little settings or collections of things that I can enjoy all about my work space. I have managed to keep one room as a "sacred cow." None of my family goes there except when we are entertaining. I have to have things around me that are beautiful."

I asked Miriam what excited her most when she was creating and she said it was color. She is likely to find a bit of something in her fabric drawer and go from there. "I build as I go, I pull out this and that . . . 'Oh, wouldn't that be nice?' and off I go." In beginning her modular doll she fell in love with the green and white stripe that she used for the legs. She avoided too much planning because she wished to be totally free.

MARINDA STEWART

When I first went to the big wholesale quilt show in Houston, Texas, Marinda Stewart was everywhere. She was everyone's helper and everyone knew who she was because she wore her Tee Dress which she had developed to hold her beautiful punch needle embroidery. I learned that she came from northern California and taught at the quilt shop that I loved and that she was very kind and giving.

As it became apparent that clothing was going to be one of my gimmicks, and knowing that fitting was never going to be my strong suit, I looked to Marinda to help me make one of her Tee Dresses. This I thought would solve all of my problems. It would cover me with lots of marvelous fabric, and once I mastered it I would never have to worry about the intricacies of fitting again. We met on a Wednesday afternoon to plot a dress. By Friday of that same week I debuted in a black Tee Dress (with three doll legs dangling down the front of it) in a fashion show which was moderated by that lively lady. I have never dressed the same again.

Marinda's needlework career began at the age of eight when she learned to embroider like her foremothers. By the time she was eighteen she was earning part of her living by custom sewing. She drifted from her love of handwork into antiques for awhile but came back with a passion and a new skill—Russian punch needle—for which she became famous. A commission to make a shirt for John Denver spread her reputation across the country, and she began to travel and teach classes.

When I asked Marinda what gave her the greatest satisfaction she told me it was solving a problem. Her approach to design starts immediately with the fabric. She confessed that if she makes preliminary sketches of a garment the finished piece often bears no resemblance.

Marinda has a reputation for being able to take strange stuff and think of wonderful things to do with it when no one else can. Her clothing and her style impart a great sense of fun and so it went—to no one's surprise—with her doll play. Lots of strange stuff stuffed into a transparent plastic casing. Things you wouldn't believe. But there they all are inside that charming doll, wrapped up in a wonderful boa ready for a night on the town. Not unlike her mother.

VIRGINIA ROBERTSON

Several years ago Virginia Robertson took her Osage County Quilt Factory to Overbrook, Kansas. Virginia had built her business in her home in Topeka, and it had become such a success that she had to find a larger place. In Overbrook she found a Methodist congregation that was also looking for a bigger place and agreed to sell Virginia their old meeting house.

I have played with Virginia Robertson in her church basement. It ranges clear across the building. There are eight and sometimes ten tables down there and you know the adage, "A woman will take up as much space as is available." Well, it's true. We decided to design a quilt using all of our dolls as appliques. We selected fabric from her 3,000 bolts stored in the sanctuary of the church. We cut off ½ yard pieces of everything we thought we could possibly use and took off to the basement to draw up a storm. Now that is play, and although Virginia claims that she had walking pneumonia and felt as sick as a dog, I remember the time as one of the all-time highs of my life.

Virginia playing by herself moves like a whirlwind. Once inspired, she can design and produce in a week more than most of us can do in a year. Her background as a teacher of drawing and painting at Idaho State University gives her work a wonderful freedom and excellent design. Her things always seem to have a fresh look.

Years ago when I first went to the wholesale quilt market in Texas, Virginia met me in her booth. There she stood with the only dolls in the entire market. Gradually the market has caught up with her, and folks are beginning to validate her farsightedness in creating dolls. There was a while, however, that she had to downplay her dolls and feature her quilts instead. My request to do a doll for this book brought her back to dollmaking. "It felt so good to play in my old laces," she said. But returning was a little painful as well. It didn't really become fun until she plunged in and the play took over.

Dolls are now a part of her life again and I for one am delighted to have played a part in bringing Virginia back.

NORMAN ENG

I met Norman in his home, which is a grand place to meet an artist because so much of him is revealed there. The cupboards were crowded with collections of things. I saw the Christmas collection and several others; and because I was an especially appreciative audience Norman brought forth one of his dolls, a clothes pin bag which was so delightful that I cradled it in my arms until I left.

Norman, a teacher of high school art for 25 years, is first-generation Chinese. He was born in Spokane, Washington, and majored in art at Washington State College, now a university, and got his masters degree in papermaking at Reed College. His great love is collage, which is the gathering of diverse elements and arranging them in such a way as to see them as new.

When I asked him what inspired the doll he made for the book, he told me that he remembers playing with his mother's button box as a child. He also had known a bag that held buttons and was embroidered with figures with buttons for faces. In the spirit of those bags of buttons, he created his lady doll. Her face, in sepia line drawing, looks old to fit the other images he used, and she could very well have been a button bag herself.

When I called to interview him, Norman told me he was just then in the process of changing a bedroom into a study. He was sponging the walls with subtly-blended colors. He and his wife Bernice love the visual and are excited by seeing the things around them change. In the study will go yet another collection, this one of things Native American. I can hardly wait to get back to Portland to have another look.

MARY MASHUTA

"Do you use a ¼″ seam on this thing?" This is Mary Mashuta.

"I've tried not to make any rules, kiddo," I said. But this was not the answer Mary wanted to hear. So I told her yes, to absolutely use a scant ¼″ seam and she went on to tell me that this was no five-hour project and it certainly did not come under her definition of fun. It will not surprise you to hear that Mary Mashuta has a great number of accomplishments, nor that every talent has its project and every piece of fabric its assignment. There is one area, however, in which Mary is unbridled. She is willing to counsel with anyone who needs her help, and she is endlessly supportive of her fellow quilters. This I know from my own personal experience.

With an extensive background in home economics, Mary is well equipped to deal with elegant needlework. Simply sewing at the machine gives her pleasure. Her beautiful quilts have been exhibited and published all over this country and in Japan as well. She has taught throughout the United States and in Canada and in addition to all this she has managed to write a book: *Wearable Art For Real People*. The list of projects that she has her hands on is very long indeed.

After explaining to me how she approached her doll, all about the hand-dyed fabric by Stacy Michelle and the pearls left over from an Yvonne Porcella workshop, and the pair of tights at Macy's that inspired the hair, she concluded. . . . "My play is pretty serious. I have to make that time count. I am on a tight schedule, and I have many things to accomplish, many obligations hanging over my head. This makes that play time pretty fruitful because my creativity is turned on all the time, so I don't have to spin my wheels trying to turn it on."

First Doll: Last Doll is the name she gave her creation. We can hope that from time to time Mary will slip again into the third dimension and join us dollmakers one more time.

ANTONETTE CELY

Antonette Cely's dolls look like her—intentionally. Inspired originally by Japanese dollmakers and with nowhere to turn for a pattern of the perfect body shape for her costumes, sylphlike Antonette chose a convenient model, herself. Using her own measurements on a ¼″ scale, she developed an elaborate method for making tiny dolls to clothe with elegant garments.

Her background as a costumer in off-Broadway theater and her love of detail and history, in addition to her childhood passion for dressing Barbie dolls, led her to dollmaking. To such an artist, obsessed with intricacy, my simple pattern and an offer to play were a bit upstream. People who are compulsive in their own direction do not find it easy to climb off the horse they are riding. But armed with her considerable sense of humor she thought she would give this no-net wire-walking a try. As I examined my own inclination towards freedom from restraints I wondered how I would have fared had our roles been reversed and she was offering me a challenge.

"I have two personalities," said Noni, "my business and professional side and my play side that dominates when I am alone or with friends. When I am making a doll, I just start. . . . Not too much planning. I test ideas for hours with painful experimentation."

I thought at first that experimentation was not the sort of play I had in mind. But then I remembered my own intense children (some were intense and some were not) and I decided that play for one person was not necessarily play for another. Noni went on to say that "problem solving, the challenge, is what's fun. No two dolls alike. My dolls are play, not work." Then she remarked, "What I enjoy doing I get paid for too."

Although Noni feels that what she does is never easy and that unlike Lisa Lichtenfels, her good friend and fellow member of NIADA, she is always conscious of the pencil and works hard at being a designer. The results are tiny masterpieces of antique grace and charm. Like Noni herself, they are close to perfection and very lovely.

3/4 yd. for body and legs ... Work with cotton

Body
1 - Cut out body from any flesh tone or color you can think of.
2 - Stitch body with two rows of stitching, one on top of the other. Leave open at the bottom. Clip, turn and stuff lightly into hand so you can top stitch fingers.
3. Stuff to elbow and make a stitched joint. Stuff to shoulder. Make an additional stitched joint.
4. Stuff head firmly and take particular care to stuff neck by holding stuffing in place to prevent it popping out at you or migrating.
5. Continue to stuff body. Turn in raw edge at bottom and pin.

fold

stitched joint

stitched joint

Stitch FELT

Breasts
1 - Hand gather around breast and stuff. Draw gathering thread close until it looks the way you think it ought to.
2. Tack gather in place to hold.
3. Press breast into body and tack along edge of breast fabric to hold in place.

fold

GATHER

HAND

Breast
CUT 2

Body
CUT 2

open

open

☆ . There was no way to avoid shrinking the pattern of the modular doll 65% - So just take her to the printer and blow her up again. Try to control yourself though. If she becomes too over-whelming you'll have to charge rent.

TACK

Leg
CUT 4

FACE

Stitch

Legs
1 - Cut legs out of whatever comes to mind.
2. With right sides together, stitch Leg. Leave open at top to turn and stuff. Clip, turn and stuff to knee. Pinch the two seams together and tack by hand or machine, thus creating a knee.
3. Continue to stuff to the top.

stitch

To Attach Leg
1. Turn doll body upside down. Set leg into body and, using crochet string, stitch back and forth until legs are firmly in place.

© 1990 elinor peace bailey ...

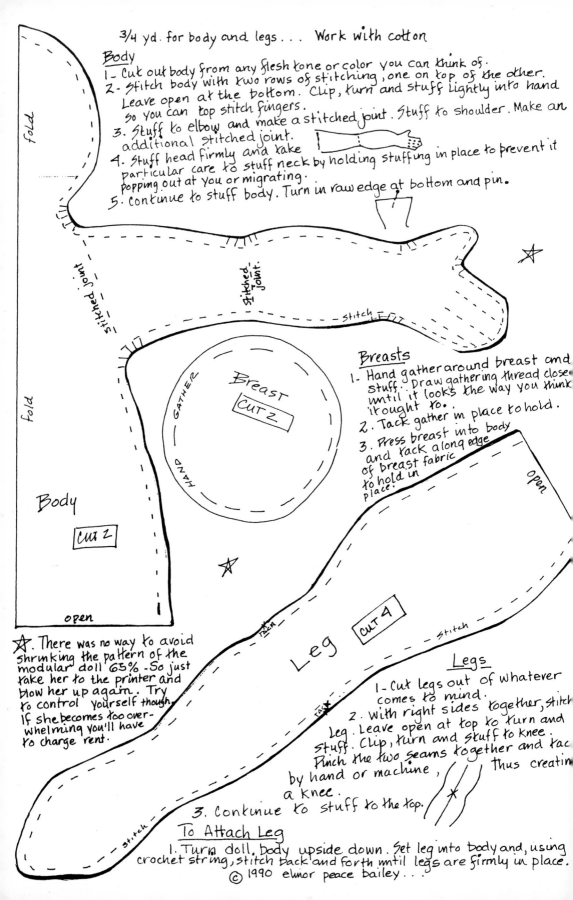